THE BATMAN STRIKES! ®

Raintree is an imprint of Capstone Global Library Limited, a company incorporated in England and Wales having its registered office at 7 Pilgrim Street, London, EC4V 6LB - Registered company number: 6695582

First published by Raintree in 2014
The moral rights of the proprietor have been asserted.

Originally published by DC Comics in the U.S. in single magazine form as The Batman Strikes! #8.
Copyright © 2014 DC Comics. All Rights Reserved.

Ashley C. Andersen Zantop *Publisher*
Michael Dahl *Editorial Director*
Sean Tulien *Editor*
Heather Kindseth *Creative Director*
Bob Lentz *Designer*
Tori Abraham *Production Specialist*

DC COMICS
Joan Hilty & Harvey Richards *Original U.S. Editors*
Jeff Matsuda & Dave McCaig *Cover Artists*

ISBN 978 1 406 28565 9

Printed in China.
18 17 16 15 14
10 9 8 7 6 5 4 3 2 1

British Library Cataloguing in Publication Data
A full catalogue record for this book is available from the British Library.

THE BATMAN IS ON FIRE!

BILL MATHENY ....WRITER
CHRISTOPHER JONES ....PENCILLER
TERRY BEATTY ....INKER
HEROIC AGE ....COLOURIST
PAT BROSSEAU ....LETTERER

**BATMAN CREATED BY
BOB KANE**

FIREFALL

WRITER – BILL MATHENY
PENCILLER – CHRISTOPHER JONES
INKER – TERRY BEATTY
LETTERER – PHIL BALSMAN
COLORIST – HEROIC AGE
EDITOR – NACHIE CASTRO
BATMAN CREATED BY BOB KANE

46...

47...
48...

...49.
50...

FEEL
THE BURN!
51...

BRRING

HELLO?
YEAH. IT'S
ME...

...FIREFLY.

NOW, CAN SOMEONE HAND ME A *BROOM?* I'D LIKE TO BE ABLE TO STOP BY HERE IN A WEEK OR TWO AND BUY SOME FLOWERS!

DO YOU THINK THAT FIREFLY IS ENGAGED IN MORE *INDUSTRIAL ESPIONAGE* THIS TIME AROUND?

NO. FROM WHAT I OBSERVED, IT'S PROBABLY A SERIES OF STRAIGHT *ARSON* JOBS. HAND ME THAT GAUGE, PLEASE.

SOMETHING TELLS ME THAT YOU'VE RULED OUT A CASE OF SIMPLE *INSURANCE FRAUD.*

THE SAME COMPANY MADE THE HIGHEST BID ON EACH PIECE OF LAND. *TRIANGLE INVESTMENTS.*

GOTHAM IS A LARGE CITY, SIR. IT COULD PROVE DIFFICULT TO LOCATE FIREFLY BEFORE HE STRIKES AGAIN.

I MODIFIED A SET OF *THERMAL SENSORS* TO DETECT INTENSE HEAT PATTERNS, LIKE THOSE FROM HIS WRIST LASERS.

TRIANGLE INVESTMENTS

MMM HMM. DIFFERENT OWNERS, EACH ONE GOOD CITIZENS. THEY CAN'T AFFORD RE-BUILDING, SO THEY'RE SELLING THE LAND.

AHH. WEREN'T THEY LINKED TO SIMILAR CROOKED PRACTICES AS YOUR OLD BUSINESS NEMESIS, *GOTHCORP?*

LINKED, BUT NO WRONGDOING WAS ESTABLISHED. *UNTIL NOW.*

17

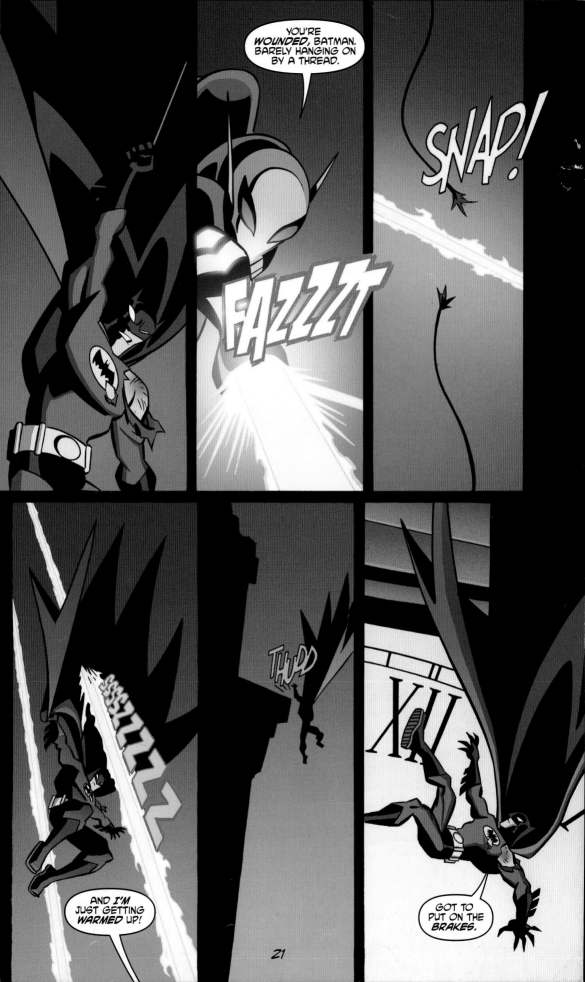

CREATORS

BILL MATHENY WRITER
Along with comics such as THE BATMAN STRIKES, Bill Matheny has written for TV series including KRYPTO THE SUPERDOG, WHERE'S WALDO, A PUP NAMED SCOOBY-DOO, and many others.

CHRISTOPHER JONES PENCILLER
Christopher Jones is an artist who has worked for DC Comics, Image, Malibu, Caliber, and Sundragon Comics.

TERRY BEATTY INKER
Terry Beatty has inked THE BATMAN STRIKES! and BATMAN: THE BRAVE AND THE BOLD as well as several other DC Comics graphic novels.

GLOSSARY

anticlimactic   if something is anticlimactic, then it seems far less important or dramatic than expected

arson   the crime of setting fire to something

assess   to evaluate or take stock of something

concur   if you concur, you agree

endures   survives or lasts through a process

espionage   the activity of spying

fraud   the crime of using dishonest methods to take something valuable from someone

mandatory   required by law or rules

revel   if you revel in something, you take great satisfaction from it

unsavoury   unpleasant in taste or smell, or disagreeable

VISUAL QUESTIONS & PROMPTS

1. Why do you think the comic book's creators chose to have Batman's Batarang overlap the panel's border here?

2. Why are there sound effects, or SFX, in this panel? Describe the various things that happen in this single panel.

...HANG ON AND SHUT UP!

SMASH KKRUNCH WHUDD KRUNCH KSSHHH CRASH

3. Batman's night vision allows him to see in the dark. In what ways does this give him an advantage against criminals?

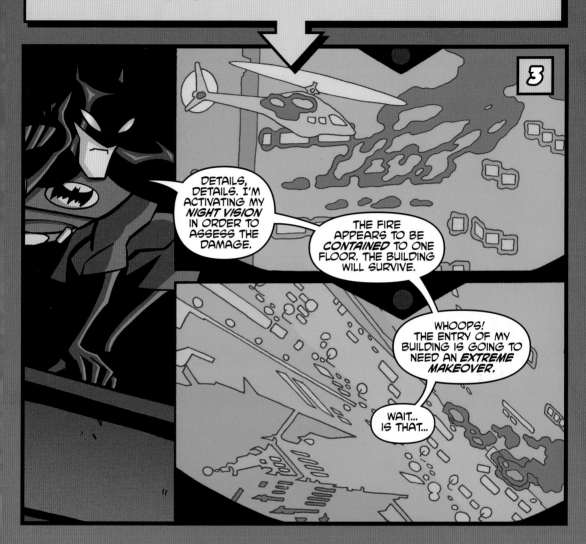

4. Batman takes down Firefly by attacking his power pack. What are some other ways the Dark Knight could have beaten Firefly?